Tindale Crescent
& Fylands Bridge

by Tom Hutchinson

Left: Tindale Crescent Hospital volunteers at the 100th anniversary of it opening. The hospital didn't officially open till 1900, but patients were accepted from the previous year.

From left to right: Susan Mason, Mary Lloyd, Olive Collinson, Mary Hodgson B.E.M., Jean Askwith, Millie Robinson, Margaret Clarke, Yvonne Richardson, Helena Hebden, Lily Hodgson, Nellie Bowser M.B.E., Lilo Davidson. These ladies worked tirelessly over the years to support the hospital, the staff and the patients (c. N. Echo).

Previous page: Brantwood Terrace – top end, c.1930s. The name Brown grocers appears in all the trade directories from 1894 to 1937. Beyond the gap is Tindale Crescent (the street).

Front cover, middle photograph: Henry Barker, Fylands Bridge, c. 1908. Henry had been born at Fylands in 1890 and at the 1911 census was working down the pit as a brakesman. He was one of a family of 12 living in Fylands Bridge House at that census. *Other photographs, from top left*: John & Colin Raine, West View, c. 1949. Annie & Florence Nattrass, West View, c.1910. Fylands Bridge Signal Box in the 1950s. Tindale Chapel Youth Club in London, c. 1968. Railway and Shaw & Knight's, c. 1960. Stanley Rusby, S. & K. Drawing Office, c. 1943.

Copyright Tom Hutchinson 2013

First published in 2013 by

Summerhill Books
PO Box 1210, Newcastle-upon-Tyne NE99 4AH

www.summerhillbooks.co.uk

email: summerhillbooks@yahoo.co.uk

ISBN: 978-1-906721-76-3

INTRODUCTION

The first edition of the Ordnance Survey map of 1859 (with later railway additions) shows the Stockton & Darlington Railway (Shildon) Tunnel branch running over the road between Broken Back House and Fieldon Bridge. East of Fieldon Bridge junction is the connection with the North Eastern Railway branch into Bishop Auckland which would not be opened until 1863. At Fieldon Bridge are cottages by the River Gaunless built c.1838 and housing about 150 people at the 1851 Census. Near Broken Back House is a branch railway from St. Helen's Colliery passing Woodhouse Close Farm to Woodhouse Close Colliery. At Broken Back House the road from West Auckland to Bishop Auckland is intersected by a road from Shildon to Woodhouses and Etherley. Less than one mile south of Fieldon Bridge is the 1825 Brusselton incline of the Stockton & Darlington Railway which was abandoned a year earlier.

This then is the area to be covered in this book. A rural area in the mid 19th century, but which 50 years later had railway facilities, gasworks, brick & tile works, clay pits, church, chapel, school, and rows of colliery and railway company houses.

In order to keep geographical confusion to a minimum the area to the south of the railway line (and much later the Bishop Auckland by-pass road) is labelled Fylands Bridge and that to the north Tindale Crescent.

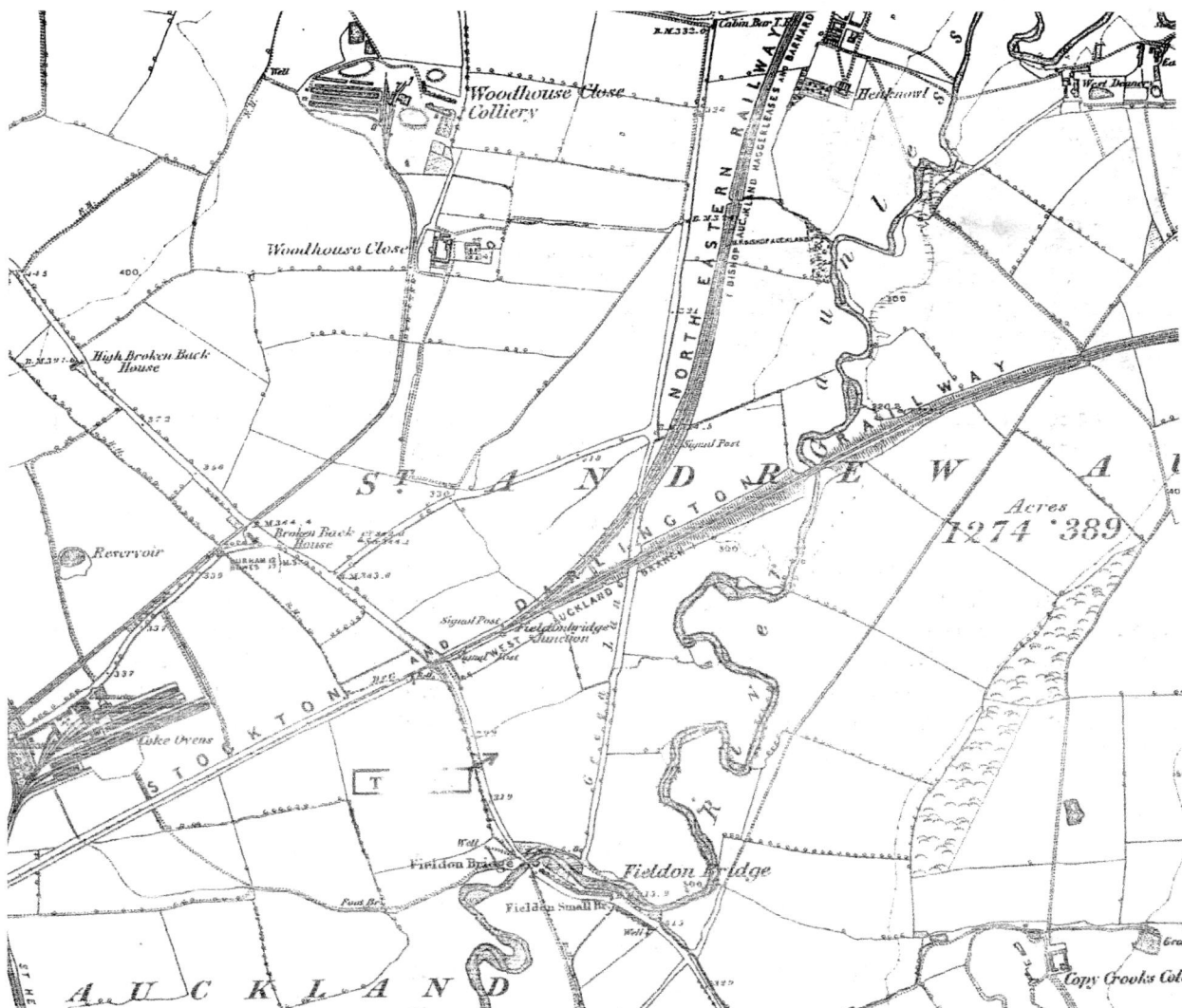

First edition of the Ordnance Survey, c. 1859, scale 6 inches to one mile. Nothing at Tindale apart from Broken Back House, and two rows of cottages at Fieldon Bridge. The farming land around Woodhouse Close Colliery and Woodhouse Close Farm was swallowed up by the building of Woodhouse Close housing estate a century later.

TINDALE CRESCENT

The first population census where individuals were identified was in 1841. At that date the only dwelling identified in the area we now know as Tindale Crescent was at Broken Back House. There at the junction of the Woodhouses road with the main road from St. Helen's to Bishop Auckland lived John Morgan, publican. According to later censuses 1851 and 1861 the house continued as an inn, but by 1871 was occupied by miners. It is said that Broken Back House had been on that site since the 16th century.

By the 1881 Census 40 houses had recently been built by colliery owners Pease & Partners for their men employed at St Helen's Colliery. The houses built of yellow fire bricks had four rooms and yards and were only five minutes walk from the colliery. It is fair to say that those houses were far superior to the 1838 houses built at nearby Fylands Bridge. The Fylands houses had only two rooms in general. After Dent Street had been built for workers at the adjacent engine shed there were 80 households identified in the 1891 Census, with over 60 of the heads of households working in the nearby colliery or on the railway. The railway engine shed had opened in 1887, along with 32 cottages and a house for the locomotive foreman. Other street names had come into existence by 1891 – Railway Terrace and Tindale Crescent (the original curved crescent of houses at the road junction). In the late 19th century further industrial development occurred in the vicinity of Tindale when the local gas company set up new works in 1881 moving their premises from the railway station approach, Bishop Auckland. At the end of that century the Cleveland & Durham Electric Power Company built a power station and depot on a site by Green Lane.

By 1901 there were over 100 houses in Tindale and street names such as Boddy Street and Brantwood Terrace appeared; supplemented by new houses in Peases Row, Hare Street and West View by the 1911 census. In 1911 there were about 600 people living in the small area bounded by the railway, gasworks, St. Helen's Colliery and main Bishop Auckland road.

The distinctive roofs of Tindale Crescent in this early 20th century postcard. The main external changes today tend to be windows and frames with some houses having porches/extensions at the front.

The following table shows the increase in the number of households in the area from 1841 to 1911:

	1841	1851	1861	1871	1881	1891	1901	1911
Broken Back House	1	2	3	4	4	4	–	5
Tindale Crescent (including Peases Houses/New Row)					32	38	37	41
Dent Street						33	33	33
Railway Terrace						7	7	7
Boddy Street							9	18
Brantwood Terrace							12	8
Hare Street								21
West View (including Back West View)								21
TOTAL	1	2	3	4	36	82	98	154

N.B. – In the days before addresses used by the Royal Mail came into standard use, the census enumerators put in addresses themselves – which may occasionally lead to difficulties in identifying locations. I think the above is accurate! It was in the 1881 census that the name Tindale Crescent first appears, but I'm unable to say where it originates. The 1897 Ordnance Survey map spells it Tindle.

The bottom end of Brantwood Terrace. The postcard has 1936 written on the reverse, but many cards show images up to 20 years earlier, so this shop may belong to S. & M.E. Dufton who were shopkeepers in the first three decades of the last century followed by Margaret Heslop in the 1940s. Today residents may remember it as Sayers.

Hare Street was built in the first decade of the 20th century. Note the distinctive bay windows compared to the earlier houses in Tindale Crescent and Brantwood Terrace. Now called Greenfields Road.

FYLANDS BRIDGE

On the first edition of the Ordnance Survey map of 1859 the two bridges over the River Gaunless are spelled "Fieldon Bridge," though the North Eastern Railway junction further north is written as "Fieldonbridge." The various censuses from 1841 to 1911 has spellings "Fylingbridge, Filingbridge, Fyling Bridge," with "Fylands Bridge" coming into usage in 1871. The Ordnance Survey were still using the term "Fieldon" until 1982.

In her Durham University thesis of 1940 called "The Derelict Villages of Durham County" Vera Temple writes that Fylands (or Fieldon's Bridge) consisted of two rows of low colliery houses, 41 in all, strung along the road from Tindale Crescent to Shildon, and were built in 1838 by Luke Simpson for workmen at Coppy Crooks Colliery less than one mile to the east.

Richard Smith with his niece Dorothy Stephenson outside no. 2 Fylands (First Row) c.1939/40. He was in the Durham Light Infantry in the Second World War. The cap's a bit big!

There was also a bigger house by the river bridge called Bridge House. She goes on to contrast those cottages unfavourably with the later ones built at Tindale Crescent from the 1870s and 1880s. Originally the Fylands houses were stone dwellings with ladders to the upper storey. The end house (no.26), complete with cellars, was to be a public house, but the licence was never obtained. The houses were later converted into two-roomed houses and inside staircases added. The end house had three rooms.

The censuses from 1841 to 1901 indicate no other residential development at Fylands apart from four families from 1881 living at the brickworks south of the railway and east of the road. The number of households in the miners cottages varied from a maximum of 44 down to 40 at the various census dates, suggesting some building alterations as mentioned above. The census of 1911, however, identifies eight new terraced houses known as Dilk (later Dilks) Street just south of the brickworks. The owner of the brickworks living in Brickyard Cottage in 1911 was Joseph Dilks, brickmaker. Four of these three-roomed houses were occupied by employees at the brickworks including the foreman.

Census information on Fylands Bridge is as follows in households:

	1841	1851	1861	1871	1881	1891	1901	1911
Fylands Bridge	42	40	43	44	42	42	42	42
Brickworks					4	1	1	1
Dilk Street								8
TOTAL	42	40	43	44	46	43	43	51

In 1911 Fylands had 26 households in First Row and 15 in Second Row, plus Bridge House.

Temple describes the Fylands Bridge houses as situated on low-lying marshy ground beside a smelly river and a clay pit. At the Tindale end of First Row she refers to an evil smelling clay pit being filled in with refuse from Bishop Auckland. Her only positive comment was that the front of the houses had a pleasant aspect towards Brusselton. Second Row houses were on the other side of the road towards Shildon and faced north. In the 1930s there were about 225 people living in those two-roomed houses and

55% were children. The houses were condemned as unfit to live in after the Second World War and the residents were rehoused in Shildon (boundary changes in the late 30s transferred land south of the River Gaunless to Shildon) in 1953/4.

However, there is an opposing view. In 1959 Elizabeth Roberts who had been the headmistress at Fylands Bridge School for four years in the 1920s wrote in the Northern Echo 'Hear All Sides': "It was once a wonderful community amidst a hive of industry … Most of the houses in Fylands Bridge and its neighbour, Tindale Crescent, were a picture of cleanliness and neatness. The weekly routine of scrubbing, polishing and scouring was a ritual never ignored. The window boxes in summer were a blaze of colour with their flowers and even blooms around the doorsteps … cannot fail to remember the wonderful kindnesses, neighbourliness and real friendship amongst this small community with its social life centred round the little St Luke's Church and the chapel."

The rear of First Row at Fylands Bridge on 1 April 1954. By that date most of the houses were derelict – the residents having moved to the Jubilee Estate, Shildon. Note the close proximity to the River Gaunless and the "outside facilities." (c. Beamish Museum).

Right: Fylands Bridge School, c.1920. Alan Armstrong arms folded in light pullover of First Row, Fylands is middle row 3rd left.

COAL MINING

Neither Tindale nor Fylands had coal mines within the boundaries of the communities, but both of them developed in parallel with the mines around them. Indeed both Woodhouse Close and St. Helen's collieries were also known as Tindale at various times.

There was a colliery at Woodhouse Close in 1800 owned by Sir Thomas Clavering, but modern records date from 2 June 1835 when sinking commenced of the North (or Engine) Pit from the surface to the Main Coal seam. This was won on 7 January 1837 when good coal was found at 74 fathoms. On 2 December 1850 sinking commenced at

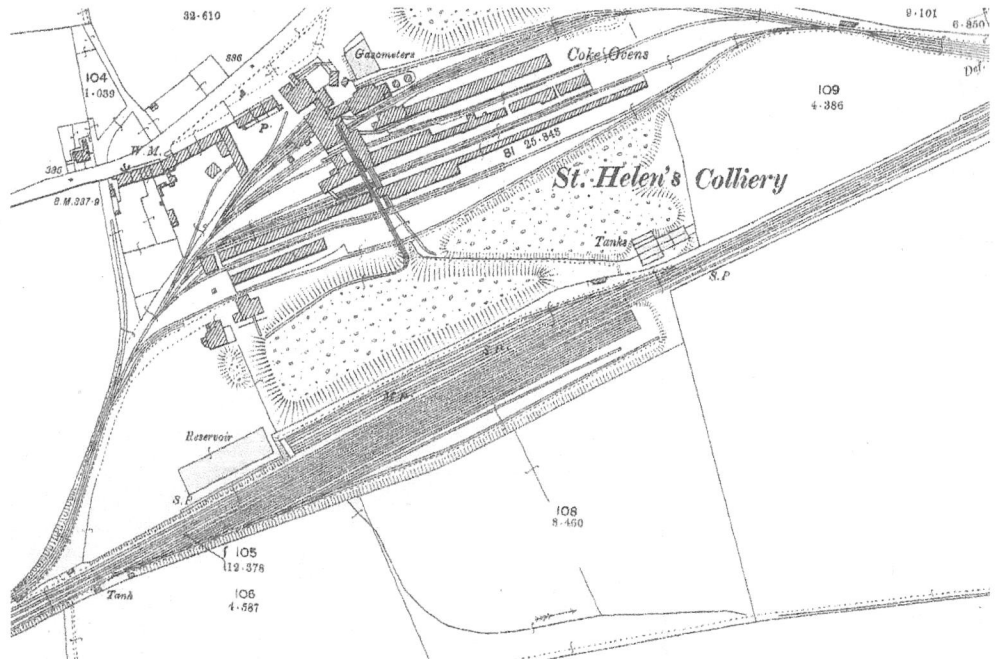

St. Helen's Colliery, 1897. Scale approx. 15 inches to 1 mile. Note the extensive railway sidings and coke ovens.

the South Pit from a depth of 15 fathoms to the Main Coal seam, and sinking started in 1854 to the Yard (Harvey) seam. The colliery was also used to take coals out of Copy Crooks Colliery about a mile away. Early owners were Vaughan & Co., Middlesbrough ironmasters, but by the 1880s, after a closure, was being worked by Pease & Partners. The owner in 1896 was William Wilkinson of North Bondgate, Bishop Auckland. It was reported closed in 1907. It was never a big pit, employing 31 men in 1896, 12 in 1927 and 93 in 1930. It closed in March 1934 when the Hutton seam was abandoned by the Woodhouse Close Colliery Company. The early owners had built a small number of cottages next to the pit as follows according to the census household returns:

1841	1851	1861	1871	1881	1891	1901	1911
2	3	10	11	10	12	7	12

It seems probable that a number of the residents of Tindale worked at Woodhouse Close. The pit site disappeared when Woodhouse Close housing estate was built in the 1950s.

Hare's Sketch of St. Helen's Colliery, 1844.

Copy Crooks Colliery east of Fylands was sunk in 1835 to the Brockwell seam, but there is little evidence of much coal being produced before 1852. Again, this was a small colliery with only 39 being employed in 1896 at the new Copy Crooks No. 1 pit nearer the Shildon road. There were 49 employed in 1914 and 36 in 1940. Many of those living at Fylands Bridge would have originally worked at Copy Crooks.

The one large colliery near to Tindale Crescent was St. Helen's which opened in 1831 after successful borings on Sir George Musgrave's Estate. Pease & Partners operated the colliery from the early years well into the 20th century. The Engine Pit was sunk to the Brockwell seam in March 1830 and the Emma Pit to the Yard or Harvey seam in October 1831. Later the Catherine Pit was sunk to the Brockwell seam in March 1835. The colliery, its coke ovens and railway sidings extended to the road at Tindale Crescent and many of the miners in the late 19th and early 20th centuries lived there. The St. Helen's colliery railway was built from the foot of the Brusselton incline of the Stockton & Darlington Railway and extended before 1850 to Woodhouse Close Colliery. In 1896 there were 386 men working at the colliery when

View of the colliery from Maude Terrace, c.1920. On the right is the office and weighbridge; beyond the winding gear and chimney.

the annual output was 120,000 tons and there were 65 coke ovens. In 1914 696 were employed and 168 in 1925. The colliery closed on 31 December 1926 and was dismantled about four years later. The site became a trading estate in 1937. The only visible colliery legacy was the wood-covered pit heap which only disappeared 60 years later.

Left: St. Helen's Colliery demolition, c. 1930. Left is Fred Moses next to William Harrison.

St. Helen's Colliery Institute F. C. 1909-1910. Back row, left to right: Jack Welsh, Moses Chapman, Tommy Hindmarsh, Billy Craggs, Bob Newton, Freddie Scott, Jack Scott. Middle row: Harry Steele, Percy Little, Tommy Shotton, Percy Oates, Tot Bagley, George Joblin. Front: Ernie Grey, Wylam Blenkin, Harry Brown. A number of these men served in World War One, and tragically Percy Little and Wylam Blenkin were killed.

TINDALE WORKMEN'S CLUB & INSTITUTE LTD

The club was formed in 1908 and was originally accommodated in premises on the north side of the main road next to Railway Terrace at its junction with the road to Woodhouses. Before that the only social premises for working men was the reading room provided by mine-owners Pease & Partners at Fylands Bridge. The club joined the CIU (full title Working Men's Club & Institute Union) in 1911 and appeared in Kelly's Trade Directory in 1914 when John Clayton was the secretary and Thomas Halfpenny the steward. In a community with no public house it is fair to say that Tindale Crescent Club (as it became later) became the centre of the local area's social life. A foundation stone was laid on 8 July 1922 of new club premises on the east side of Tindale Crescent next to allotment gardens. The new premises opened in 1923 at a cost of £12,000 had a concert hall, bar, lounge, offices and committee room. By that time Thomas Turpin was the secretary and Charles Thom the steward. Indeed Charles Thom who had been in the licensed trade at the Highland Laddie, Bildershaw and the Locomotive Inn, St. Helen's before World War One remained at the club until his retirement in 1940 - about 25 years. The 1946 Electoral Roll shows John Stephens living in the steward's house at the club. In the 1950s the building of the large Woodhouse Close housing estate nearby, brought an influx of new members. By 1981 according to a newspaper report 'Club Chat' there were 1500 male members, 230 life members and 700 female members who enjoyed the enhanced facilities of a concert hall, bar, lounge, offices and committee room, and very supportive of charitable events, children's summer outings and Christmas festivities, particularly for the life members. The club celebrated 100 years of membership of the CIU on 8 September 2011.

Taking the air outside the club in the 1930s are left Wilf Howson, William Edward Armstrong and Dick Dobson.

Left: Charles Thom, wife Mary and daughter Flora in the bar of the new club, c.1925

Right: Tindale Committee in front of the new premises, c. 1925. Back left: C. Thom, steward, J. Dodds, A. Martin, J. Simpson, J. Ratcliffe, R. Mason, L. Brown. Front left: J. Thubron, T. Turpin, secretary, D. Davis, chairman, G. Baker, treasurer, H. Bradley, T. Walton.

Tindale Committee, 1950. Back left: R. W. Peareth, J. A. Robinson, J. Armstrong, W. Ormston. Front left: T. V. D. Berg, G. W. Guy, treasurer, A. Martin, president, E. M Dodds, secretary, R. Walton.

Tindale Crescent WMC Touring Club summer outing 1964. Standing back, left to right: Ticky Longstaff, Jimmy Ross, Ernie Siddle, Freddy Lowe, Roy Musgrave, Charlie Jennings, Harry Vickers, Ronnie Howe, Stan Rutherford, Norman Thompson, Mickey Barker, Billy Barker, Matt Adams. Front left: Bill Hutchfield, George Copeland, Eddie Dawe, Myles Hunt.

Tindale WMC who won the "grand slam" in 1976 – League, League Cup and Darlington Charity Cup. Back left: Ronnie Savage, Dale Daniel, Colin Smith, Brian Hardy, John Lang, John Shaw, Eddie & Robert Sharp, Michael Grady, Chris Shield. Front left: Ray Hutchfield, Bobby Latcham, Colin Mills, Johnny Hussey, George Richardson, John Latcham, Jackie Foster, Colin Bly. Mascot – Michael Grady.

Presentation evening of Bishop Auckland & District CIU in 1977. Tindale WMC football team with their trophies. Back left: Dale Daniel (sec.), Michael Grady (man.), Ray & Billy Hutchfield. Front: Alan Iceton, Jackie Foster (capt.), Billy Hardy.

Pigeon racing presentation night, c.1970s. Left: George Gaskill, Dennis Egglestone, Norman Gilroy, ? ?, Margaret Smith, ? ?, ? ?, Kevin Bryan, June Egglestone, Fred Crawford, Ray Belton, Joe Crawford.

KELLY'S TRADE DIRECTORY 1914

Auckland, Shildon & Willington Joint Hospital Board Infectious Diseases Hospital –
Miss E. Francis matron.
Fylands Bridge C. of E. School (Infants), 104 children, Mrs H. Smith mistress.
John Baines, saddler.
Gas Company – George W. Young manager.
A. Brown & Sons, grocers.
Wm. Brown, greengrocer.
Electricity – R.H.Jenkins resident engineer.
S. & M. E. Dufton, shopkeepers.
George Flower, carter.
Emily S. Hindmarch, shopkeeper.
John Hutchfield, shopkeeper.
George Pearson, fried fish dealer.
Post Office – Charles Coulthard.
Samuel Thompson, confectioner.
Tindale Workmen's Club & Inst. Ltd. – John Clayton, sec., Thomas Halfpenny, steward.
H. R. Vaughan & Co. brickmakers.
Lily Welsh, shopkeeper.
John Wilson, confectioner.

YOUNG PEOPLE

A long time ago, c. 1918 – George Pedelty, Bert Middlewood and Norah Pedelty outside the rear of 18 West View.

A 'cheeky' picture! Neil Bacon and David Ward, c. 1957.

The Askwiths and Horsmans of Peases Row were long time family friends. A picture from 1959. Back left: John and Judith Askwith, Hilda Horsman. Front left: Harry and Margaret Horsman.

Left: On the slide for Colin Jeffery's birthday, September 1977. Dog Tiny with Colin; children: Hutchfield cousins – Robert, Julie & Tracy, Bainbridge sisters – Nicola & Karen, Bailey brothers – Robin and Paul, Darren Simpson, Mark Richardson, Christopher Raine.

15

WEST AUCKLAND ENGINE SHED

This railway engine shed was opened in 1887, having been authorised by the North Eastern Railway in December 1885. The shed itself was of typical North Eastern Railway pattern with 18 "roads" round a 50 foot turntable and two entrance roads. Eventually within the confines of the shed were offices, stores, mess room, sand drier and steam raisers fire. Outside was the coal stage, old canteen which was later used as a classroom, wooden store and cycle shed.

It is a mystery why it was called West Auckland as it was further away from that village than the much larger town of Bishop Auckland. It was also called Fieldon Bridge or Fylands Bridge locally. The estimated cost of £17,650 also included 32 cottages and a house for the locomotive foreman. At the 1891 census the cottages – called Dent Street – were all occupied by railway employees in occupations such as drivers, stokers (firemen) and guards at the shed. There were 53 employees of the railway in those houses out of a total of 218 inhabitants with the two senior men being Edward Black, locomotive foreman at 1 Dent Street and Henry Evans engineer & foreman at number 2. Those houses at the 1901 census had 7 rooms each, so perhaps the North Eastern Railway had some building alterations done from the original plans. By 1911 the locomotive foreman at number 2 was William Thirkell, but at number 1 was Charlotte Black, widow. By then three of the houses had no railway employees living there, but there were still 48 railway workers living in the street. Some of the families had lived in the street at least 20 years by 1911 – the following surnames may be familiar – Bainbridge, Cockfield, Littlefair, Murray, Thrower, Wearmouth, Walker, Winston. Indeed the Thrower family were still living in Dent Street in 1980. The vast majority of the houses had five rooms and would be seen as attractive propositions a century ago.

Right: Engine shed in 1954. John Askwith has identified the photo from left to right: * back roads some formerly leading to St. Helen's Colliery with pit heap at the back. * time office in left hand corner of shed – sand dryer top left side, stores top right, canteen right hand corner. * coal loading facility.* 'in' road to shed, with 'centre' road holding a wagon collecting ashes, 'out' road from shed.

* stores building and bike sheds. There was a small area in front of the stores building where buffers were stored (three men standing about there). John used to sit on these and watch the locomotives being coaled and ash dropped. In the old coach education and training classes were held.

Most of the railway guards identified in the various censuses were guards on mineral trains. In 1922, for example, the shed supplied only one daily "passenger turn" which required two sets of men and took them to Ferryhill, Barnard Castle and Stockton. In that year there were 22 locomotives based at West Auckland and 102 men. As an economy measure in the Great Depression the shed closed on 13 April 1931 and most of the 16 locomotives were transferred to Shildon. Four years later it was decided to close Shildon and Wear Valley Junction sheds and to reopen West Auckland from 8 July 1935 with an initial allocation of 15 locomotives including five sentinel railcars. The shed staff took over all mineral trains over Stainmore summit to Cumberland and also provided men and locomotives for passenger services to Darlington, Durham, Ferryhill, South Shields and Wearhead. The Second World War brought more duties to the shed and by 1947 35 locomotives were based there, increasing to 46 in 1954. Monthly the shed provided locomotives for the Durham coal miners special taking them to a convalescent home in Ulverston, Lancashire, and also the summer Saturdays Newcastle to Blackpool trains.

The rundown of the shed started in 1957 when diesel railcars took over local passenger duties and the closure of the Stainmore line in 1962 brought further rationalization. Local collieries and railway goods depots were also closing and the announcement of the shed closure was to be on 7 September 1963. A new stabling and train crew depot was to be set up at Shildon, but this was not ready by the September so West Auckland shed eventually closed for the second and final time on 3 February 1964 when there were 12 steam locomotives allocated to the shed. The last duties were on the previous Saturday 1 February when two steam locomotives and one diesel left the shed as follows:

No. 77010 – Stanhope goods pick-up. No. 63446 – light to Darlington.

No. D5174 diesel from Brancepeth to ICI Haverton Hill coal train.

The site was eventually cleared in 1965 and a cash & carry warehouse established c.1970, with Hathaway Roofing moving into a factory on the site in 1975. The Bishop Auckland by-pass obliterated any remains of the surrounding environment of the shed in the 1990s.

Men in 1960 photograph in front of standard class 4 locomotive no. 76021. Back left Gordon Reed boilersmith. Middle left: Vic Alexander storeman, Jock ? Darlington electrician, Joe Hopper steam raiser, ? Bayles fitter's mate, Fred Piercy fitter, Stan Johnson coal stager, Allan Orton fitter's mate, Ken Walker timekeeper. Front: Harry Hope shedman, Ray Humble fitter, Roy Thomas boilersmith's mate. (c. G. Reed).

The water crane and class J27 locomotive no. 1029 form the backcloth to the six men relaxing for a photograph in this Second World War scene. From the top: George Stephenson, Les Bainbridge, Isaac Lee (?), Arthur Watson, Joe Hall, Harold Bacon.

Left: Three locomotives grouped round the turntable in this late 1950s view. Left Q6 class no. 63407, middle class 4MT no. 76045 and right J26 class no. 65735.

TINDALE ELECTORAL ROLLS
1946 & 1980

(spellings as written)

BODDY STREET 1946 — 1980

1946	1980
1 Lilian Hall, Robert & Nellie Hedley	Norman & Greta Chambers
2 Albert & Ivy Wilson, Annie Maria Smith	Colin & Stella Jones
3 William, Selina & Alma Stevens	Colin & Vera Mills
4 William & Gladys Toase, Robert Simpson	Ronald Ellison, Doreen & Stephen Kelly
5 Oliver & Jane Hodgson, Stanley Cole	Mabel Clarke
6 Sydney, Margaret & Elsie Shipp	Margaret Shipp
7 James Ogilvie, Ruth Asquith	Reginald & Brenda Gelding
8 Thomas & Mary Conroy	Mary Wilson
9 George, Louisa & Elsie Harper	Edward & Sandra Baker
10 James Howes, Joseph & Sarah Close, William & Elsie Thorburn	William & Mary Thompson
11 Victor & Elizabeth Simpson	Terry & Ruby Tallentire
12 Thomas, Hannah, Rose, Sarah & Agnes Conroy	
13 Mary & Jane Booth	Kelvin & Mary Morley
14 Thomas, Margaret, Elizabeth & Annie Hemsley	Margaret Helmsley, Frederick & Annie Watters
15 Roy & Martha Walker	Colin & Ann Richardson
16 William & Theresa Liddle	
17 James & Ivy Holmes	Charles & Margaret Elliott
19 William & Eva Simpson	(18/19) Eva Simpson
20 Henry & Mary Battes	

BRANTWOOD TERRACE 1946 — 1980

1946	1980
1 Christopher & Margaret Heslop	Harry, Marjorie & Carole Sayers
2 Thomas & Selina Ward	Keith & Linda Chapman
3 Richard & Margaret Toase	Richard Toase
4 James & Lucinda Baker	James & Lucinda Baker
5 Percy & Hilda Slack	Percy & Hilda Slack
6 Walter, Elsie, Maurice & Frances Stephenson	Walter & Elsie Stephenson
7 Laurence, Murial, Granville, Ronald, Percival & Margaret Mills	Joseph & Marjorie Blenkiron
8 John & Ada Glasper	William & Mavis Mundell
9 Leslie & Ruth Brown	Georgina Arbuthnot
10 William, Florence & Sarah Arbuthnot, James Steward	Olive Bailey
11 Alan & Elizabeth Hall, Theresa Cole	
12 Ethel Baines, Mary & Ethel Page	Trevor & Dianne Million, Colin & Yvonne Jeffrey
13 Thomas & Nora Cutler	Francis & Joan Simpson
14 Richard & Mona Dobson	Graham Bosson

BROKENBACK COTTAGES 1946 — 1980

1946	1980
2 Robert & Alice Emmerson, Norman & Florence Dent	(1/2) George, Jean & Steven Brassell
3 George & Mabel Thompson	George Harrison

DENT STREET 1946 — 1980

1946	1980
1 Fred, Betty & Lilian Dobson	Raymond & Betty Saville
3 John & Elsie Hutchinson	John & Elsie Hutchinson
5 Percy & Harriet Tarn	Harriet Tarn
7 Frank & Meggie Hunter	Kenneth, Maureen & Lee Warburton
9 Ernest, Elizabeth, John & Elsie Murray Joseph & Phyllis Wright	George & Anne Brown, Mary Speed
11 Thomas, Gertrude & Raymond Wood	Paul & Theresa Waites
13 Alfred, Margaret, Alfred (jun.), Norman, George & Annie Thrower	Alfred, George & Harry Thrower
15 Alfred, Lydia & Ethel Toase, Lydia Shoulder	Ethel Toase

17 George & Ruby Johnson	Ralph, Jean, Ralph & Mandy Raine
19 William & Annie Spence	Harold & Lucy Prest
21 Mawson & Emma Hutchinson, Alfred Howlett	Alan & Christine Makinson
23 Raymond, Harriet & George Turnbull	Anthony & Lynne Stephenson
25 Smith & Sarah Henderson	Ronald, Sheila, Malcolm & Brian Watson
27 George & Mary Guy, John Walton	Henry, Vera & Wendy Watson
29 Arthur, Emma, Frederick & Mary Ratcliffe	Edwin & Katrina Armstrong
31 Robert & Gladys Walton	Colin & Christine Binks
33 Jane Hutchinson	Jane Hutchinson
2 James, Florence, Cuthbert & Jean Middlewood, Mary Jane Nattrass	Joan Waine, John Chopin
4 Margaret Scott, John Oliver	Margaret Scott
6 John & Sarah Hutchinson	Thomas, Agnes & Brian Harbron
8 Joseph & Annie Wilkinson	Robert, Doreen & Wendy Newton
10 Henry & Elizabeth Walton	Alan & Gwynneth Gordon
12 Matthew & Elizabeth Brown	Reginald, Georgina & Graeme Eales
14 John, Sarah & Marjorie Binks, Cyril & Florence Morland, Mary Mothersdale	George & Theresa Binks, Sharon Yahya
16 Florence & Joyce Ward	William & June Ward
18 Matthew & Frances Storey	Ronald Bacon
20 John & Hannah Robinson	George & Christine Guy
22 Ralph & Nora Crawford	John, Jean & Norman Ornsby
24 Ralph & Olive Grainger, Elizabeth Johnston, Ruby & Wanifred Bayes	
26 Robert & Henrietta Peareth	Joseph Harvath
28 John & Gladys Hall	Alan & Sheila Harrison
30 John & Edith Dixon	Florence Bainbridge
32 Thomas & Isabella Barugh	Donald, Irene & David Hogg

PEASES ROW (PEASE STREET)

1946	1980
1 Reuben Parkin	Jean & Judith Askwith
2 Adam & John Nichol, Spencer & Marg. Clarke	John & Lyn Dowson
3 Tobias Vandenburg, Florence Mothersdale, Eva Coates	Joseph & Phyllis Fairless
4	Laurence & Edith Raine
5 Alfred, Margaret & Joseph Beadle	Robert, Lilian & Julie Bailey
6 Thomas, Maggie & Jane Dixon	Charles & Edith Jennings
7 Mary Ann Craggs	George & Brenda Longthorne
8 James & Martha Dixon, John & Margaret Crawford	George & Joyce Blackburn

WEST VIEW 1946

1946	1980
1 Thomas & Martha Iceton, Wilfred & Mary Bateman	Alma Edwards
2 Donald & Doris Barnard	William Milliken, Margaret Bainbridge
3 Robert & Alice Ventress, Edwin Lee	Robert & Annie Ventress
4 George & Mary Flowers, David & Mary Ross	Norman & Hilda Thompson
5 Florence Heslop, Ellen Baul	Frank, Geoffrey & Barbara Longthorne
6 John & Jemima Richardson	Jemima Richardson
7 Charles & Laura Walton	George & Winifred Douthwaite
8 Sarah Ann Bainbridge	Samuel Arbuthnot
9 Henry & Beatrice Horsman	Gibson, Mary & Linda Raine
10 Stanley & Doris Hull	Doris, Denis & Joyce Hull
11 Gibson & Mary Raine	John & Edith Norris
12 Norman, Mary, Douglas & Francis Brown	Joseph, Joan & Graham Robson
13 Albert & Violet Howe, James King, George Wetherell, Robert & George Coulthard, Leslie, Daisy & Thomas Vickers	Charles & Daisy Carr, Thomas Vickers, Terry & Gillian Armstrong
14 John & Ruth Gills	Norman & Gladys Moody
15 William & Annie Moses	Annie Moses, James Allinson

16 Elsie Brown	Wilfred & Olive Middlemas
17 Frederick & Louisa Thubron	Dowson Hymer
18 George, Hilda & Thomas Beadle	James & Mary Wedmore
19 James, Sarah & George Pedelty	Grace Sowerby
20 Jacob & Nellie Hedley, Elizabeth Plant	Ann Wicks ?
23 ?	Mary Coulthard

TINDALE CRESCENT (+ Railway Terrace)

1946	1980
1 Robert Glasper	Raymond & Catherine Hutchfield
2 George & Theresa Binks	Florence Sayers
3 Beatrice & Ada Currey	David & June Wright
4 John, Mary & Elizabeth Sowerby	James & Margaret Duffy
5 James & Rose Crawford, John Holmes	Rose Crawford
6 William & Isabella Glover	Elizabeth Keleher
7 Mary Elizabeth Robinson	Joseph Mulholland
8 John & Dinah Armstrong	John & Dinah Armstrong
9 William & Elizabeth Armstrong	Alan, Ivy & Trevor Armstrong
10 Frederick & Violet Wynn	Beatrice Gilbey
11 Stanley & Lavinia Robinson	Anthony & Barbara Metcalfe
12 Joseph, Annie & Albert Close	Annie Close
13 Ernest & Elizabeth Firby	John & Patricia Bayles
14 Sam., Mary & Arth. Brown, Robert & Ellen Aither	Philip & May Tarn
15 Ellen Vickers, John & Ellen Glasper	William Vickers, Ellen Glasper
16 Miles & Sarah Woodward	Kevin & Elizabeth Smith
17 Charles Robinson, George & Bertha Hodgson	George & Bertha Hodgson
18 George Pearson, Samuel & Ada Brown	
19 Richard & Mary Bradley	Nora Wood
20 Louisa Liddle	Stewart & Marian Lowe, Lorna Wood
21 Beatrice Hodgson	Beatrice Hodgson
22 George & Sarah Hodgson	Michael & Lynn Stead
23 Fred, Eleanor & Arnold Wood	Ralph, Lily & Anne Padgham
24 John & Isabella Wood	George, Hilda, Harry & Margaret Horsman
25 Elizabeth, Frances & Anthony Martin	Thomas & Grace Ward
26 James & Grace Ward	

(RAILWAY TERRACE – 1946)	(TINDALE CRESCENT – 1980)
1 Emily Hindmarch, Robert & Violet Garbutt	26/27 Thomas & Dorothy Johnson
2 George & Irene Foster	28 Roderick, Cicely & Margaret Davies
3 William & Cicely Hodgson	31 Derrick, Jean & Derrick (jun.) Hopper
4 Robert Hull, Mary Gills	
5 George Nattrass, Ethel Robinson	

HARE STREET/ WHEATSHEAF ROW 1946	GREENFIELDS ROAD 1980
1 Joseph & Jane Jennings	
2 George & Emma Morgan	1 Barrie & Julie Morgan
3 Joseph & Elizabeth Bowron, Elizabeth Schofield	
1a Douglas & Florence Heughf	3 Beryl Rose
1 Elizabeth Hare	7 Jack & Margaret Dobson

HARE STREET 1946	GREENFIELDS ROAD 1980
2 George & Hannah Wilkinson	9 Raymond & Lilian Spence
3 John & Elizabeth Wright	13 William Greenwell
5 Albert & Phoebe Gladwell, Vera Alderson	15 Albert Gladwell
6 Alfred & Ethel Lockey, Elizabeth Cumbor	17 Alan Hodgson
7 Jonathan Dodd	19 Allison & Stella Makepeace
8 Alexander & Lucy Rennie	21 Thomas & Ivy Dobson
9 Raymond & Sarah Carter	23 Olive Goodfellow
10 John & Marg. Reeve, Norman & Gladys Moody	

11 Richard & Hannah Adams
12 Alan, Kathy & Maud Saxby
13 Allan & Sarah Toase
14 William & Nora Simpson
15 John & Cicely Weatherill
16 Mary Thompson, Olive Noble
17 Margaret Vaughan
18 Henry & Elizabeth Jameson
19 Margaret Dunn, Stanley &
   Norah Richardson
20 John & Elizabeth Flowers
21 Parker & Annie Booth
22 Norman & Olive Goodfellow

27 Hannah Adams
29 Trevor, Agnes & Shaun Vickers
31 Sarah Glass
33 William & Norah Simpson
35 Alan & Susan Moore

39 David & Edith Stephenson
41 Francis & Mary Cruddace
43 William Coltman

45 John Flowers
47 Peter & Joyce Oughton
49 William & Lynn Howe

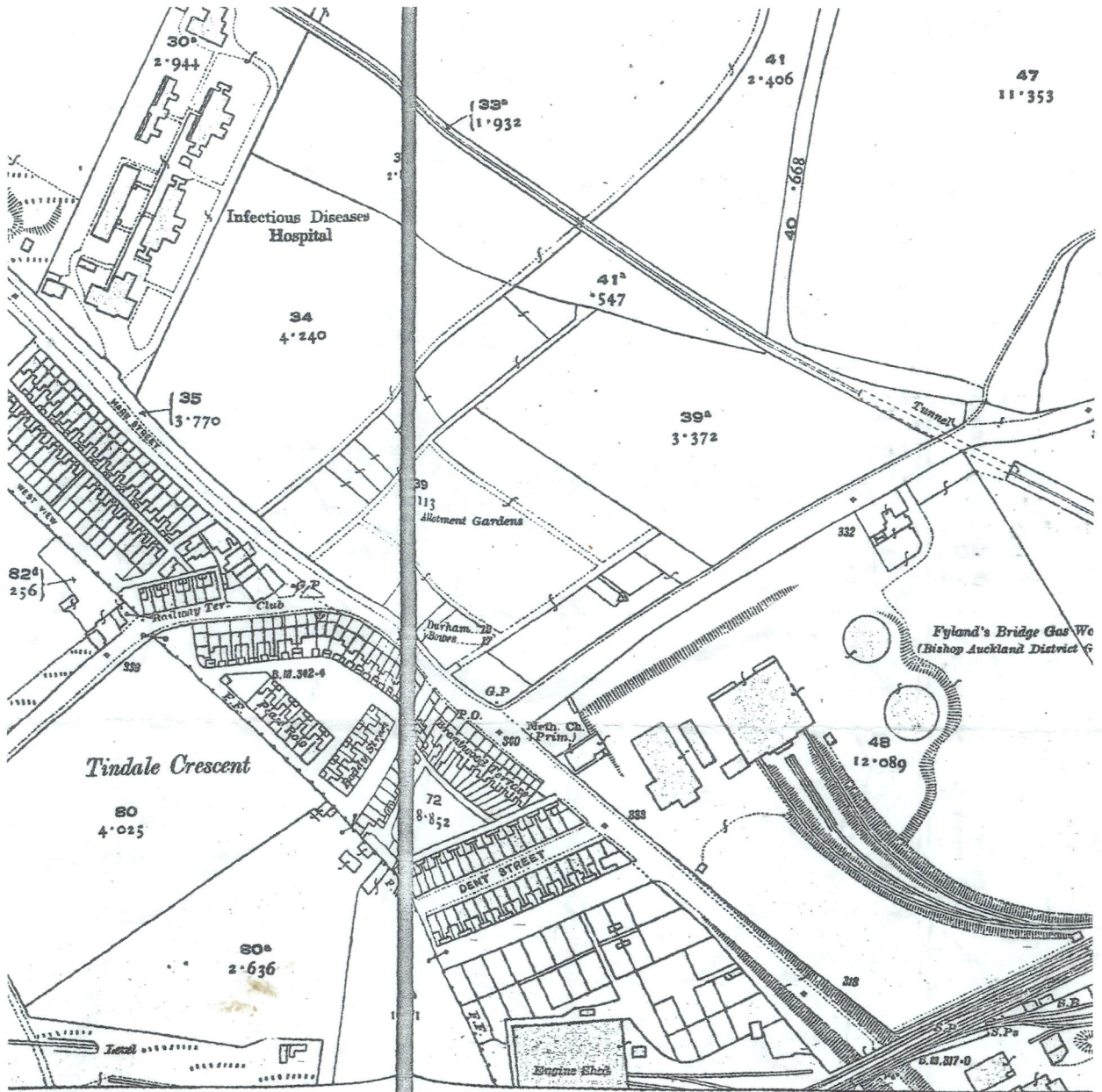

Tindale Crescent 1920, scale 25 inches to 1 mile. The road running east from the end of Railway Terrace across the allotment gardens to cut out the dog leg change of direction for road traffic was not built until later in that decade. The railway siding and tunnel under the main road was still in existence going behind the isolation hospital to Woodhouses Colliery. The siding from St Helen's Colliery to Woodhouse Close Colliery had been removed. Note the large area covered by the gasworks.

HOLLYWOOD BEAUTIES & OTHER TALES OF FYLANDS

The bachelor girls of Fylands 1937. First left: Vera Smith, 4th Lilian Smith, 6th ? Hodgson, 8th Violet Smith. Who were the others? (c. N. Echo)

In 1937 the Auckland Chronicle reported that the unmarried girls of Fylands felt that their prospects of marriage were blighted by living in the village which, they said, had been shunned by Cupid. Boys refused to escort them home from dances in Bishop Auckland or Shildon. As the girls outnumbered the boys by two to one in the village, they felt that they might be left "on the shelf." The girls decided to alter the name of the village to "Hollywood" and soon proposals of marriage reached the village from all over! Eventually, all the girls took marriage vows – but to local lads!

In April 1954 the same newspaper went back to report that "Hollywood" had been condemned and that already half the homes were empty. Where once lived mining families now only remained empty shells with holes in place of windows and doors. The community south of the River Gaunless eventually disappeared and the 1990s altering of the road from Tindale to Shildon means that it is difficult to find evidence of where the two rows of houses stood from 1838 to 1954.

Syd Stephenson remembers as a child in the 1940s:
* Gas lamp lit the living room and water was heated in a boiler to the side of the coal fire.
* Baked bread and scones cooling on the large fender surrounding the hearth.
* Bathing in a cold wash house in a long, narrow galvanised steel bath.
* Playing marbles, digging small holes and marking out the boundaries in the dirt road.
* The "beck" was our swimming pool and made the water deeper by building a dam.
* Village pond freezing over and people from all round coming to skate on the ice.
* One small shop only selling sweets, liquorice, bootlaces and odds & ends in the front room of Dunbars at number 20.
* During the 1947 winter snow nearly reached the top of telephone poles in the fields.
* Wilf Taylor who lived in no. 1a butchered his own pigs, curing the bacon, boning and rolling the sides and hanging them up in the pantry wrapped in muslim netting.
* Annie Smith, Syd's grandmother served as the village's midwife, gave out dressings and bandages, and laid the deceased out. She also kept geese and a pet magpie, and was the last to leave Fylands after 40 years. Her husband was a miner who drove a pony & trap to the pit at Chilton and also had an allotment, stables and sheds.

By the early 1950s though:
* Mrs Whitworth was living in a house having only one (upstairs) room in which to eat, sleep, bath and do her washing for five children.
* Mrs Armstrong who lived downstairs from Mrs Whitworth could push a letter through cracks in the wall to next door.
* Their means of lighting were candles.
* Five families shared one ash closet.

FYLANDS C. OF E. INFANTS SCHOOL

The school opened in 1891 at a cost of £350 to accommodate 70 children. This was to cater for housing developments at Fylands and Tindale Crescent. There were two classes at the end of which children went either to St. Helen's the old British School – or from 1909 to Cockton Hill School. This was a small school compared to St. Helen's which took up to 265 scholars. It was built in association with the nearby church of St. Luke's which opened in 1882. By 1914 the head mistress was Mrs H. Smith in charge of 104 children. A similar number were at school in 1925 when Miss H. Armorey was in charge.

Right: Fylands School, c. 1952 taken from the road and across the yard.

The school over 75 years ago in 1936. The little boy immediately behind the middle of the shield is Jackie Dobson. The Dobsons who originally came from Kirkby Stephen worked for the North Eastern Railway and lived in Dent Street.

Fylands School Christmas Play, c.1946. Left: Billy Close, Russell Clarke, George Ross, Peter Noble, Marlene Slack, Arly Garbutt, Sylvia Hunter, June Ward, Hughie Foster, Audrey Barker, Joyce Winn, Elsie Peareth, David Ross (c. Northern Echo).

The demolition of the two rows at Fylands in 1954 and the building of Woodhouse Close housing estate from the mid 1950s with the development of schools, churches and shops in that estate meant that the future of Fylands School became bleak, and the school closed in the early 1960s. The site was eventually cleared and today nothing remains of the school.

25

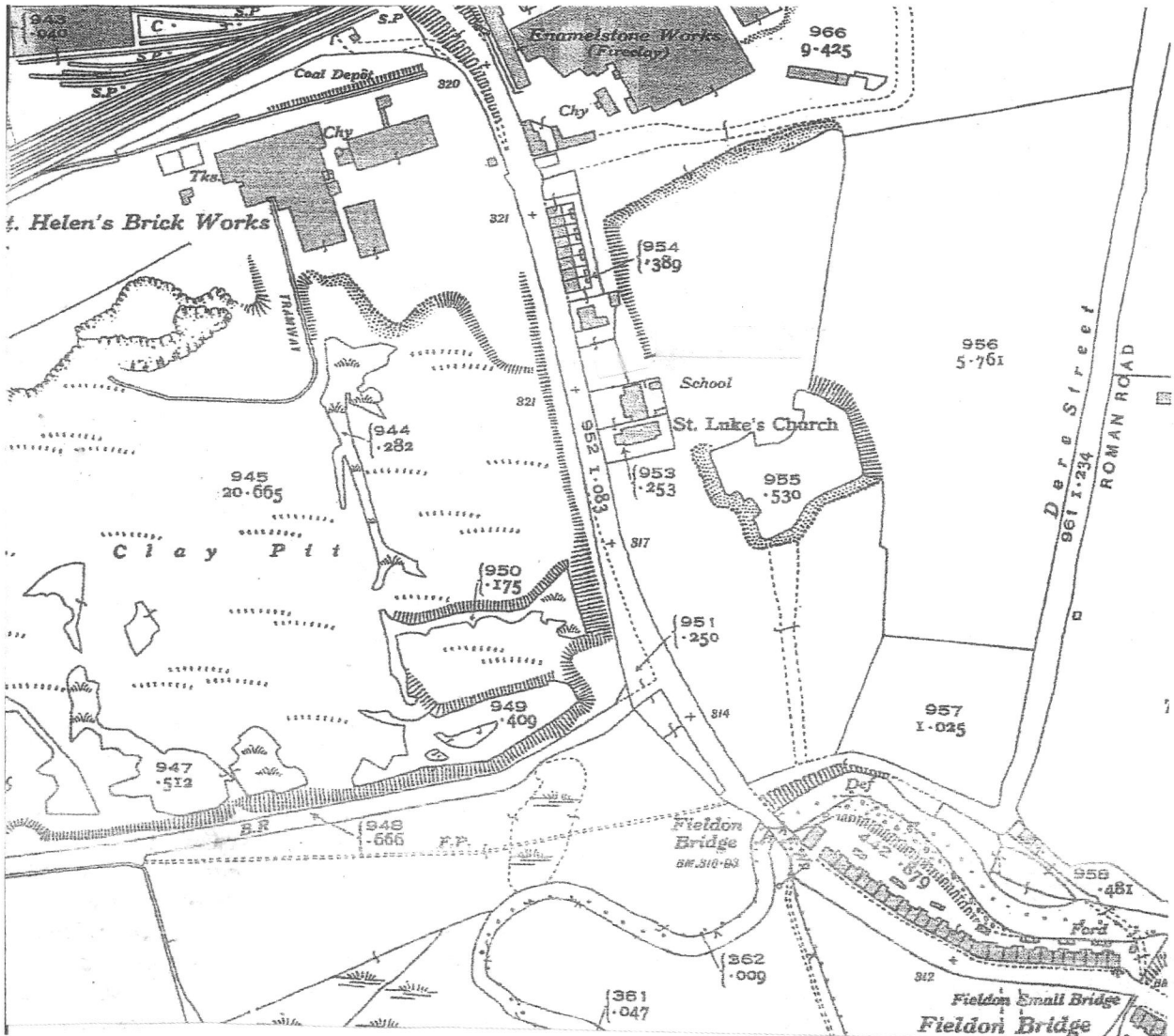

Fylands in 1939, scale 25 inches to 1 mile. Many people will remember the area south of the railway before the War. East of the road was Shaw & Knight's enamelstone works, to the west the brickworks owned by H.R.Vaughan & Co. – later used by Stephenson's contractors as a depot. Also shown is St. Luke's Church with Fylands School just north of it. At the extreme south end beside the road is the first row of houses at Fieldon Bridge (note the spelling) with the rear of the houses near the south bank of the River Gaunless. The second row of houses just starts to appear on the opposite side of the road next to Fieldon small bridge. Note the extensive clay pits to the west of the church.

Photograph of a house interior in one of the rows at Fylands on 1 April 1954 gives a vivid depiction of the condition of the 115 year old dwellings just prior to demolition. This is one of the first floor premises with no ceiling to the room and open up to the rafters – very cold and damp as can be seen particularly to the right of the fireplace. The washing hanging from a string slung between the rafters (c. Beamish Museum).

RELIGIOUS PREMISES

Whellan's Directory of 1894 mentions St Luke's Chapel at Fylands Bridge and the Primitive Methodist Chapel at Tindale Crescent both built in the same era when the area was still expanding to cater for the influx of labour into the mines, railways and brickmaking. St. Luke's is described as a neat brick building with accommodation for about 120 and was used as a chapel of ease to St Andrew's (South Church). The parish registers date from 1882 to 1966. The Primitive Methodist Chapel at Tindale dates from 1886, built of brick to seat nearly 200 at a cost of £425, including purchase of the site opposite Brantwood Terrace.

The Methodist Chapel, c. 1937.

Both churches served the community for over 80 years, but the building of new churches on the Woodhouse Close estate meant that the older buildings became redundant. The Methodist chapel is still there today and used by a commercial firm as offices/workshops. St. Luke's suffered the fate of being used as part of garage premises for a while before being completely demolished. The site has been cleared including the garage, and associated underground petrol tanks which were filled with concrete in 1998.

A few thoughts on St. Luke's from a former member: "when War broke out in 1939 the younger congregation members were called up and the Sunday School closed as the teachers were on war work. Two sisters, the Misses Martin, who lived opposite Tindale Post Office insisted on a lay reader coming out to lead the one Sunday service. They were always to be seen on Sundays walking down to church. The numbers eventually dwindled to closure. It was used as a car workshop for a short time and then was demolished. A few children from the Sunday school started to attend services at St. Helen's. Some of the adults went to the newly built church at Woodhouse Close."

St Luke's Church in December 1967 after conversion into a garage (c. Northern Echo).

Methodist Chapel Sunday School Anniversary, 1957/58. Back row from left: Mr. Adams, Ann Cosgrove, Winston Chamberlain, Jane Middlewood, Gertie Robinson, Ruby Johnson, ? ?, ? ?, Christine Carr, Jennifer Holmes, Patricia Siddle, Trudy Williams, Betty Williams, ? ?, ? ?, ? ?, ? ?, Paul Chamberlain. The children in the front include various representatives of the Bowman, Latcham and Moses families.

TINDALE CRESCENT HOSPITAL

The chief cause of early death in the late 19th century was infectious disease – infantile diarrhoea, scarlet fever, diphtheria, measles, typhoid fever, tuberculosis, smallpox – so hospitals dealing with those diseases tended to be the first ones set up. Whellan's Directory of 1894 mentions a fever hospital established in 1885 housed in two small cottages in South Church Lane, Bishop Auckland accommodating eight patients. This building never had more than 21 beds and could only treat one type of disease at a time as all facilities were "under one roof." An unsatisfactory arrangement which would become more so when proposals that notification of certain infectious diseases be made compulsory. This became law in 1899 by which time the Auckland, Shildon & Willington Joint Hospital Board was already building a dedicated infectious diseases hospital at Tindale Crescent. The Board built a similar hospital at Helmington Row in 1908.

The Hospital Board had obtained three loans totalling £7850 between November 1898 and December 1899 for the purchase of site and erection of buildings at Tindale. On Wednesday 2 May 1900 the new hospital for infectious diseases was officially opened by Mr. Fenwick Darling. The hospital cost £7993 inclusive of site cost and furniture and covered three acres in area. A penny of the rates would more than cover the annual running costs of £865. The

The main building with foundation stone at roof level.

buildings completed by that date were an administrative block, main pavilion, isolation block, laundry block and outbathing block, but provision had been made for two further pavilions. There was also a mortuary and ambulance. A key feature was that wards were separated so that different diseases could be isolated. According to the Auckland Chronicle & Herald newspaper "all the wards are light and cheerful in every respect and have the latest improvements in heating and ventilation." The windows were double-glazed and the planners seem to have set great store in the admittance, without draughts, of fresh air and expulsion of foul air. Great emphasis was placed on the disinfecting procedures both of patients and clothing.

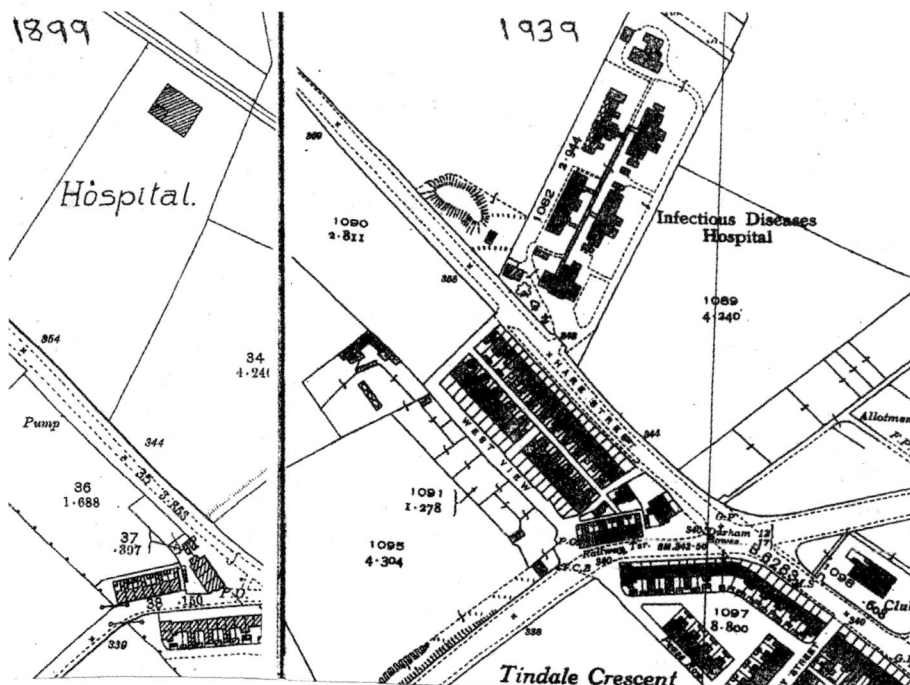

Maps showing the hospital in two eras – 1899 and 1939. There were no houses near the hospital on the earlier map. They were built in the next decade. Note also that a new road had been built by 1939, west to east, north of the working men's club to save traffic having to travel between the club and gasworks to reach Bishop Auckland.

Miss A. B. Bridges was appointed matron in charge and Dr. R. B. Smeddle of Shildon the medical officer. By 1908 three wards usually devoted to the treatment of diphtheria, scarlet fever and enteric fever (typhoid and similar) were functioning. At the 1911 census there were 17 patients – all but one under 14 years of age – in the hospital tended by matron Alice Booth, five medical and three other staff. By 1930 the hospital had 60 beds compared to 42 before the First World War and a fourth ward for pulmonary tuberculosis patients had been opened.

In 1955 the hospital which in the latter years had been treating tuberculosis patients was converted in use to become a geriatric and general convalescence hospital. The last matron Sylvia Snowdon was also appointed in that year and set about building up its facilities after the rationing of the wartime years. Staff, furniture, beds, lockers, linen and equipment were moved from the general hospital in Bishop Auckland. One significant feature of Tindale Hospital was the significant use of help from voluntary services which culminated in c.1970 with the Tindale Crescent Hospital Helpers, a group of ladies who for the next 30 years generated over £100,000 in donations by their various fund-raising efforts from starting a hospital radio, organizing summer trips and picnics for patients and providing "comforts," to the highlight of the hospital's social calendar – the annual garden party. The final garden party in 2001 raised over £1,000.

Nurses Christmas Party, c.1967. Back left standing: ? ?, Anne Livingstone, Sylvia Snowdon, Gladys Kane, Teresa Brott, Gladys Glass, ? Atkinson, Anne Burdess, ? ?, Flo Stephenson, Peggy Jones. From front left: Annie Ventress, Mary Watson (front), Anne Dixon (behind), Betty Ascough, Wynn Mitzson, Marina Cheesemond, Anne Ascough, ? ? Phyllis Fairless, Mary Mounsey, Sally South.

Changing medical views as well as the apparent conquering of infectious diseases had resulted in many small fever hospitals closing over the years, but the use of Tindale for elderly patients as well as the provision of day case chemotherapy, blood transfusions and acupuncture from 1997 meant that the hospital continued providing a valuable service until 2002. The £67 million hospital then opened in Bishop Auckland on the site of the old general hospital/workhouse, and Tindale closed.

In recent years the Tindale site has been cleared and houses called Snowdon Crescent – an acknowledgement to Sylvia. The old hospital served the community well and is fondly remembered by staff, friends and helpers.

AROUND THE COMMUNITY

Summer of '63 with Norman and John Ornsby on board class Q6 no. 63403. Not something that "ealth & safety" would allow today!

John and Isabel Dobson of Dent Street, c. 1930s. John was an engine driver for the North Eastern Railway at Kirkby Stephen and came to work at Tindale about 1920.

St. Helen's & Tindale Over 60s, c.1959. From left: Sarah Toase, Joan Holmes (only 14 then), Ivy Holmes, ? ?, ? ?, ? ?, Olive Bruce, Eva Simpson, ? ?, Margaret Shipp, Mrs Foxton.

Happy faces in Tindale Club, c.1962. Left to right: Ernie Siddle, George Copeland, Geordie Stott (standing), Charlie Jennings, Kevin Slack, Tommy Teasdale, Frank McGuinness (hidden), ? ?, ? ?

Above: Another photograph of Fylands School Christmas play, c. 1946 King – Peter Noble, Queen – Marlene Slack. Others standing includes Joe Clark, Maureen Barry, Jean Morgan, Beryl Toase. Sitting includes Hughie Foster, Jean Hodgson, Kathleen Paley, Lily Barker, David Ross. Miss Armstrong was the headmistress. (c. N. Echo).

Right: Sunday School Anniversary, c. 1950. Back left: Margaret Adams, ? ?, Joyce Hall. Front: Valerie Close, Jane Middlewood, Valerie Witt, ? ?, John Norris, ? ?

Left: Labour Party float in Tindale Carnival, c.1950. Eighth along from left on vehicle is Hilda Slack.

45

CHILDHOOD MEMORIES OF THE 1940S & '50S by JANE ARMSTRONG (NEE MIDDLEWOOD)

* During the War Miss Anne Scott, 4 Dent Street, iced cakes for family celebrations. For weddings family and friends would donate their rations for cake ingredients and icing. Miss Scott made 'icing sweets' from left over icing and put them in grease-proof paper bags for the children in the street.
* We used to sneak into the engine shed and, when no one was watching, went round on the turntable as an engine was being turned.
* We also used to sneak into the pigeon crees and try some of their food!
* My uncle Jim Pedelty was the blacksmith in the gasworks and we used to watch the sparks flying as he worked.
* Mrs Wood in the Crescent kept the 'board' to lay out people who had died.
* The Co-op sold bread in the village from a horse and cart and the delivery man for many years was Mr. Cavanagh from Witton Park. We used to feed his horse.
* The 'ash men' used to clean out the middens along Dent Street. In a similar vein the toilets, sinks and baths manufactured at the nearby works of Shaw & Knight was a fascination.
* On a Sunday School anniversary day we sang to the children in the fever hospital. We were not allowed inside so could only see the children through the windows.
* Christopher and Margaret Heslop ran the shop at 1 Brantwood Terrace. She wrote out a bill using a thick pencil that she licked before writing each word. The pencil was sharpened with an old small kitchen knife. We climbed on top of crates of pop to reach the counter. Mrs Brown's shop nearby was so dark and gloomy that we were scared to go in.
* On a Monday night after the Harvest Festival the fruit and vegetables were auctioned at the chapel. We sat at the front and were eventually given an apple.
* In the harsh winter of 1947 my friend's granddad cut huge blocks of snow to make us a snow house in the back street.
* We played a lot outside – tops & whips, hop scotch, roller skates. Long walks up to Brusselton Folly passing the 'Roman' stones on the way. In the woods there were pit shafts we dared each other to look down. We collected wild flowers in summer and berries in the autumn; climbed trees and played in the river; freedom and fresh air.

Brusselton Folly, on a postcard dated 14 October 1924, about 25/30 years before Jane knew it. An 18th century tower built by the Carr family for observation purposes – demolished half-a-century ago. Children would have walked there on a footpath called Haggs Lane along the track of the Roman road – Dere Street – from Fylands to Brusselton Hill. At the end of the 19th century the tower was surrounded by old coal shafts and quarries, with Brusselton Quarry to the west still operating.

FYLANDS BRIDGE 2013

The houses to the south of the bridge are the only residential properties that have completely disappeared in the 20th century and nearly 60 years later natural woods and grasses have reclaimed most of the area. The shell of the water tower that is sited near to the River Gaunless at the eastern end of First Row is still there along with the back retaining walls of the ash closets at the rear of Second Row. Where the bridle way from Hummerbeck Farm along Burnshouse Lane to South Church intersects the old road from Fylands to Shildon, there can still be seen a few yards of the tarmac of the old road with white road markings still visible. On the site of Second Row are a few small slag heaps hidden in the grass. In front of Second Row is pasture land so it can be envisaged where the houses stood. The site of Bridge House and the 26 houses in First Row is, particularly in the summer, hidden by the trees and long grass. Near the river hidden in the undergrowth is a stone post which was possibly at the end of the old bridge parapet across the Gaunless. A few bricks were found by the river bank – one stamped "Randolph" which may be from the ash closets which backed onto the river. The ash closets were built later than the houses and by that time bricks from Randolph Colliery, Evenwood may have been cheaper?

The rear of Second Row with the ash closets retaining wall. In the background the old water tower.

A patch of the old road north west of Coppy Crooks Farm.

Possibly part of the old bridge parapet over the River Gaunless hidden in the undergrowth by the river.

The beck which was originally straddled by Fieldon Small Bridge. First Row was to the left and Second to the right of the stream.

ACKNOWLEDGEMENTS

I and the Tindale Crescent Residents Association would like to thank the following who have helped with this book by loaning photographs, providing information and assisting in many ways:

Beamish – The North of England Open Air Museum, The Northern Echo, Matt Adams, Jean Anderton, Bill Annals, Jane Armstrong MBE, John Askwith, Sylvia Baker, Alan Bramhald, Nellie Bowser MBE, Janet Chapman, Andrew Clark, Harold Clark, Keith Cockerill, Dale Daniel, Freda & Neville Davison, Sheila Davison, Joan Dobson, Evelyn Graham, Ray & Anne Hutchfield, Colin Jeffery, Mike Keen, Tommy Kelly, Charles Lilley, Dr. Robert McManners OBE, Andrea Patchett, Doris Peacock, Gordon Reed, Kevin Richardson, Moira Robinson, John Rusby, Frank Sanderson, Joan Simpson, Kevin & Lorna Slack, Sydney Stephenson, Lynda Thom, Marlene Watson, The O.S. maps by kind permission of the Ordnance Survey.

We would like to thank Councillor John Lethbridge for the kind donation from his funds for our book.

BIBLIOGRAPHY

North Eastern Railway – W. W. Tomlinson
North Eastern Locomotive Sheds – K. Hoole
B.R. Motive Power Depots, N.E. Region- P. Bolger
The Derelict Villages of County Durham: Durham University Thesis – Vera Temple
History of Bishop Auckland – Tom Hutchinson
Directories/Gazetters between 1858 and 1937
1841 – 1911 Censuses
1930 – 1980 Electoral Rolls
Durham Mining Museum Website

The Queen's Silver Jubilee celebrations 1977. From left to right: Joanne Thompson, Deborah Thompson, Renata Iantello, Julie Wilson, Jillian Dobson.